MIND MYTHS EXPOSED!

by Megan Cooley Peterson

CAPSTONE PRESS
a capstone imprint

Published by Spark, an imprint of Capstone
1710 Roe Crest Drive, North Mankato, Minnesota 56003
capstonepub.com

Library of Congress Cataloging-in-Publication Data is available on the Library of Congress website

ISBN: 9781666357103 (hardcover)
ISBN: 9781666357110 (ebook PDF)

Summary: Readers will be captivated by claims of psychic powers while also learning the facts about each story. Exciting, easy-to-read text and compelling images will keep struggling and reluctant readers alike flipping the pages to find out.

Editorial Credits
Editor: Mandy Robbins; Designer: Heidi Thompson; Media Researcher: Jo Miller; Production Specialist: Tori Abraham

Image Credits
Alamy: Chronicle, 8, 9, 11, Colin Waters, 13, Glenn Francis, 27, Pictorial Press Ltd, 7, The Print Collector, 17, ZUMA Press, Inc., 19; Shutterstock: Africa Studio, 16, agsandrew, Cover, 2, 5, Bananaboy, 15, Biker x days, 29, Bohbeh, 23 (compass), JpegPhotographer, 25, leshiy985, 28, revers, 24, Studio Light and Shade, 23 (red ball), Taratun Maryna, 23 (matches), VanoVasaio, 12, Vladimir Hodac, 21, Yan Yarman, 20

Printed and bound in the USA. PO4882

TABLE OF CONTENTS

Words in **bold** are in the glossary.

MIND POWERS

Have you ever dreamed about something before it happened? Have you known what someone was going to say before they said it? This is called **ESP**. Some people say they can see the future. Others claim to read people's minds. Is it real or just a trick?

THE FOX SISTERS

Trouble started for the Fox sisters in March 1848. They lived in Hydesville, New York. Loud knocks woke up 14-year-old Maggie and 11-year-old Kate every night. No one knew what, or who, made the sounds. The noises followed the sisters around the house.

Kate Fox as an adult

One night, their parents tried to solve the mystery. They had friends over to help. Everyone crowded into the sisters' bedroom. They asked questions. There were knocks in reply.

They learned a man had been buried under the house. His **spirit** was trying to talk to the sisters.

Maggie, Kate, and Leah Fox

Maggie and Kate moved in with their older sister, Leah, in Rochester, New York. Leah started having **séances**. People paid money to watch the sisters speak with ghosts. The sisters became famous. They called themselves **mediums**.

FACT

The sisters claimed to speak with famous ghosts like Benjamin Franklin.

In 1888, Maggie and Kate said they were fakes. They dropped apples and cracked their toes to make the knocking sounds. About a year later, Maggie changed her story. She said they really could speak with the dead.

FACT
The sisters' former home in Hydesville, New York, is said to be haunted.

READING MINDS

Can people read each other's minds? In 1882, two men from England said they could. Douglas Blackburn and George Smith agreed to be tested. George sat blindfolded in a room. Douglas went into a hallway. He was shown a drawing of a shape.

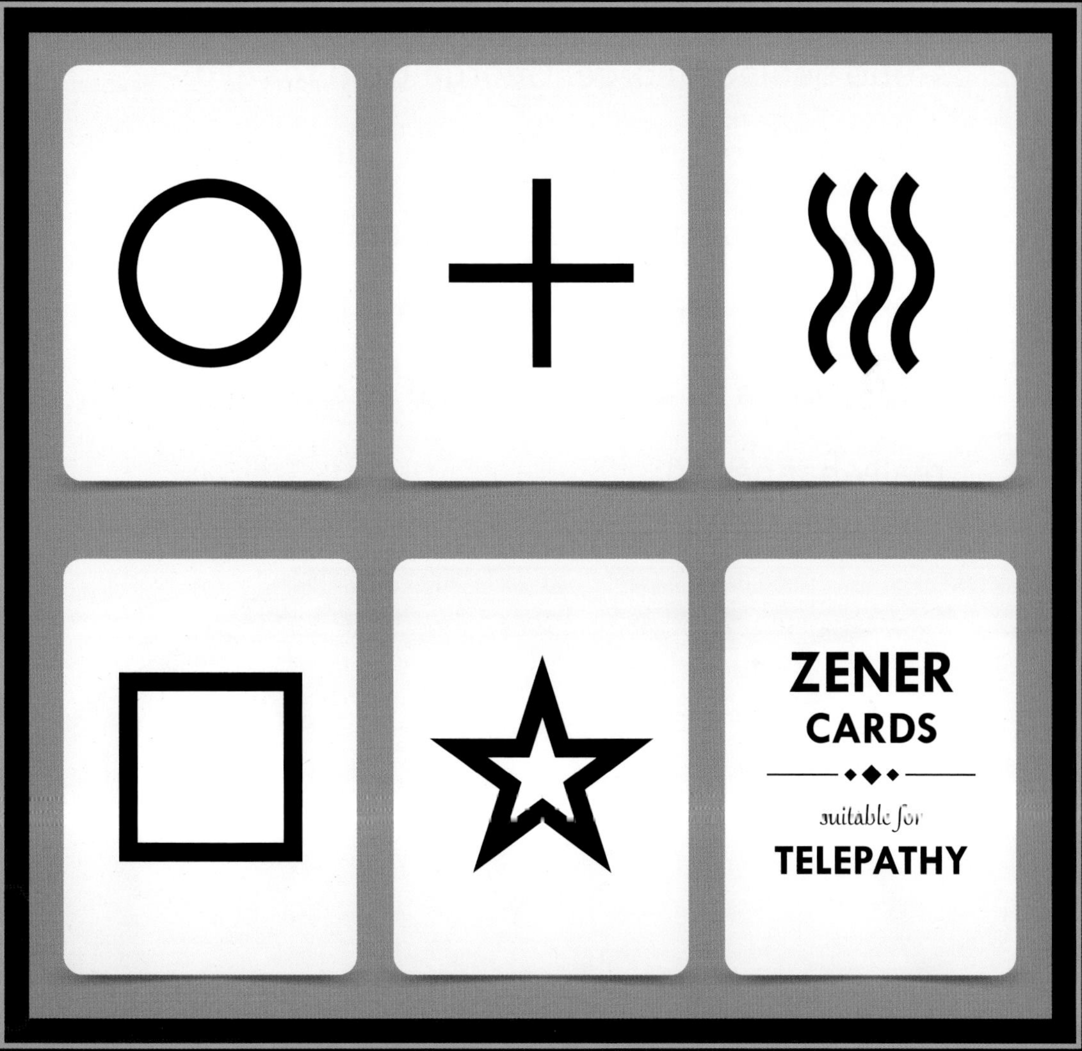
ZENER
CARDS
suitable for
TELEPATHY

Douglas went back into the room and stood behind George. George tried to read his friend's mind. Then he drew the shape on paper. Out of 37 tests, they only failed eight times. About 30 years later, Douglas said it was a **hoax**. But George said it really happened.

Mind-reading games were popular at parties in the 1800s.

SEEING INTO THE FUTURE

In 1946, an Irishman named John Godley had a strange dream. He dreamed the results of two horse races. But the races hadn't happened yet. John placed bets on those races. He hoped he might win.

FACT
John said his mother could see into the future.

John Godley with actress Jayne Mansfield

The horses he had dreamed of won their races. John dreamed about other races too. One time he wrote down his dream and sealed it in an envelope. He wanted to prove he wasn't lying.

After the race, he opened it. His **prediction** had come true. Could John dream the future? Or did someone help him cheat?

MOVING OBJECTS

Russian Nina Kulagina had a strange talent. She could move things with her mind. In the 1960s, the Soviet Union's government tested her powers.

FACT

The Soviet government made films of Nina moving objects.

Nina surprised researchers. She moved a glass, matches, and a **compass** needle without touching them. She even raised a small ball into the air.

Nina often felt tired and dizzy after moving objects. Some people thought she was faking it. They thought she used hidden magnets to move the compass needle. But there was no proof Nina lied.

FINDING MISSING PEOPLE

A plane disappeared near the coast of southern California in 2016. A student pilot and his teacher had been flying together. For days, no one could find them.

The U.S. Coast Guard called medium Fia Johansson. She had helped police for years. They hoped she could help find the plane.

Fia Johansson

Fia joined the search. She said she could feel the spirit of the student pilot. He told her the plane had crashed. He also told her where to find it. Fia led the Coast Guard right to where the plane had gone down.

FACT

Fia started working with police when she was a teenager.

the Pacific coast

Glossary

compass (KUHM-puhs)—an instrument people use to find the direction in which they are traveling; a compass has a needle that points north

ESP—the ability to gather information beyond the five senses of touching, smelling, seeing, hearing, or tasting; ESP stands for extra sensory perception

hoax (HOHKS)—a trick to make people believe something that is not true

medium (MEE-dee-uhm)—a person who claims to make contact with spirits of the dead

prediction (pri-DIK-shuhn)—a statement of what you think will happen in the future

séance (SAY-ahns)—a meeting at which people try to make contact with the dead

spirit (SPIHR-it)—the invisible part of a person that contains thoughts and feelings; some people believe the spirit leaves the body after death

Read More

Borgert-Spaniol, Megan. *ESP: Does a Sixth Sense Exist?* Minneapolis: Checkerboard Library, an imprint of Abdo Publishing, 2019.

Peterson, Megan Cooley. *Urban Legends Exposed!* North Mankato, MN: Capstone, 2023.

Polinsky, Paige V. *ESP.* Minneapolis: Bellwether Media, Inc., 2020.

Internet Sites

Do You Have ESP?
wonderopolis.org/wonder/do-you-have-esp

Easy Mind Reading & Prediction Tricks
thesprucecrafts.com/easy-mind-reading-and-prediction-tricks-4121829

ESP
easyscienceforkids.com/esp/

Index

About the Author

Megan Cooley Peterson has been an avid reader and writer since she was a little girl. She has written nonfiction children's books about topics ranging from urban legends to gross animal facts. She lives in Minnesota with her husband, daughter, and cuddly kitty.